How to Be
RESPECTFUL

A Question and Answer Book About Respect

by Emily James

CAPSTONE PRESS
a capstone imprint

Being respectful is an important part of character.

A person's qualities make up his or her character.

Respecting someone shows you
care how that person feels. You can
respect others, yourself, and even Earth.
There are lots of ways to show respect.

Elena just scored a point for her soccer team. But a player from the other team got hurt.

How can Elena show respect?

Elena stops to help the player up.

Good sportsmanship is one way to show respect.

Can you think of another way to show respect in sports?

Julia's dad makes
the family dinner.
**How can Julia
show respect
to her dad?**

Julia sets the table.

When you help out without being asked, you are showing respect.

Can you think of another way to show respect at home?

Evan borrows his friend's basketball.

How can Evan respect his friend?

Evan puts the ball in a safe place. Taking good care of someone's things shows respect.

What is another way to show respect for someone's things?

Kate's grandma takes her shopping.
How can Kate show her grandmother respect?

Kate holds the door open for her grandmother.

Doing something nice for someone else shows respect.

What is something nice you can do for someone to show respect?

Alex is visiting a friend.

How can Alex respect his friend's house?

Alex makes sure not to leave a mess.

Being considerate shows respect.

How can you be considerate to someone?

Why is being considerate a way to be respectful?

Jackson is playing a game during recess.

Some other children are standing nearby watching.

How can Jackson show respect to the others?

Jackson asks them if they would like to join the game.

Including others is a way to show respect.

Can you think of another way to show respect to others at recess?

Eli is a busy kid!

But sometimes he gets tired.

How can Eli show respect for himself?

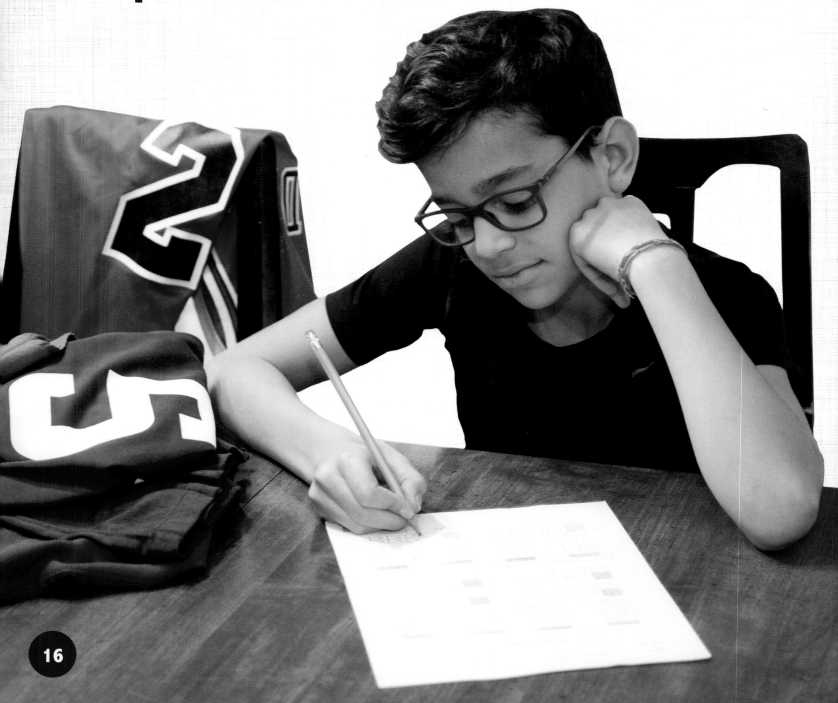

Eli gets plenty of sleep.

Taking care of yourself is very important.

Can you think of another way to take care of yourself?

Sofia is going to the park to play.

Her parents tell her to be home before dinner.

How can Sofia show them respect?

Sofia goes home before dinner. Following the rules shows respect.

How does following the rules at home or school show respect for others?

Mya walks through the lunch line at school. **How can Mya show respect to the lunch workers?**

Mya says "please" and "thank you."

Using manners shows respect.

Where else can you use manners to show respect?

Lily has a cat named Whiskers.

But her uncle is allergic to cats.

How can Lily show respect to her uncle?

Lily takes the cat to another room when he visits. Caring about someone's health shows respect.

How can you show respect for a person's health?

Colin promises to help his dad clean the house. Then Colin's friend asks if he can go to the park.

How can Colin show his dad respect?

24

Colin keeps his promise.

He does not go to the park.

Keeping a promise shows respect.

Have you ever wanted to break a promise? Why is keeping a promise respectful?

Ethan's science teacher

is talking to the class.

How can Ethan show

respect during class?

Ethan listens quietly while the teacher is talking.

He raises his hand to answer questions.

How can you respect your teacher or others during class?

Jayla asks her teacher about ways
to help the environment.
**How can Jayla show
respect to Earth?**

28

Jayla recycles her water bottle.
Helping the environment
shows respect for Earth.

How can you respect Earth?

Glossary

allergic—when something makes someone feel sick; many allergies make you sneeze

considerate—thoughtful of the needs and feelings of other people

environment—all of the trees, plants, water, and dirt

quality—a special feature of someone or something

sportsmanship—playing a sport or game respectfully and fairly

Internet Sites

Use FactHound to find Internet sites related to this book:

Visit *www.facthound.com*

Just type in 9781515772002 and go.

Read More

Higgins, Melissa. *I Am Respectful*. I Don't Bully. North Mankato, Minn: Capstone Press, 2015.

Ponto, Joanna. *Being Respectful*. All About Character. New York: Enslow Publishing, 2016.

Yankee, Kris and Marian Nelson. *Are You Respectful Today?* Becoming a Better You! Northville, Mich.: Ferne Press, 2014.

Critical Thinking Questions

1. How does Eli show respect for himself?

2. Good sportsmanship is one way to show respect. What is sportsmanship?

   Hint: Use your glossary!

3. Can you think of a time when you showed respect? What did you do?

Index

borrowing, 8

cleaning, 24

environment, 28, 29

feelings, 2

health, 23

helping, 5, 7, 24

manners, 21

playing, 14, 18

promises, 24, 25

qualities, 2

recess, 14, 15

recycling, 29

rules, 19

sleeping, 17

sportsmanship, 5

teachers, 26, 27, 28

A+ Books are published by Capstone Press,
1710 Roe Crest Drive, North Mankato, Minnesota 56003
www.mycapstone.com

Library of Congress Cataloging-in-Publication Data
Cataloging-in-publication information is on file with the Library of Congress.
Names: James, Emily, 1983- author.
Title: How to be respectful : a question and answer book about respect / by Emily James.
Description: North Mankato, Minnesota : Capstone Press, 2017. | Series: A+ books. Character matters
Includes bibliographical references and index. Identifiers: LCCN 2016057032
ISBN 9781515772002 (library binding) | ISBN 9781515772040 (ebook (pdf)
Subjects: LCSH: Respect for persons—Miscellanea—Juvenile literature. Respect—Miscellanea—Juvenile literature.
Classification: LCC BJ1533.R42 J36 2017 | DDC 179/.9—dc23
LC record available at https://lccn.loc.gov/2016057032

Editorial Credits
Jaclyn Jaycox, editor; Heidi Thompson, designer; Jo Miller, media researcher;
Laura Manthe, production specialist; Marcy Morin, scheduler

Photo Credits
All photographs by Capstone Studio/Karon Dubke, except:
Shutterstock: Monkey Business Images, 20, 21, Syda Productions,
14, 15, wavebreakmedia, 26, 27, 28, 29, RoyStudioEU,
throughout, (background texture)

Printed In the United States of America.
010364F17